THE COLORS OF
HOLI

Let's learn colors and celebrate the Indian festival!

by Amy Singh

Idika and Aakav celebrate Holi festival. It is also known as the "festival of spring" and the "festival of colors".

The festival is the symbol of the triumph of good over evil and the changing of the seasons from winter to spring.

People celebrate the festival by making frolic and color battles on the streets.

Let's see the most important Holi colors!

SAFFRON

kesar

केसर

Saffron, called "Kesari" is traditional Holi color. It is a holy and sacred color, associated with Hinduism and strength; the most important color.

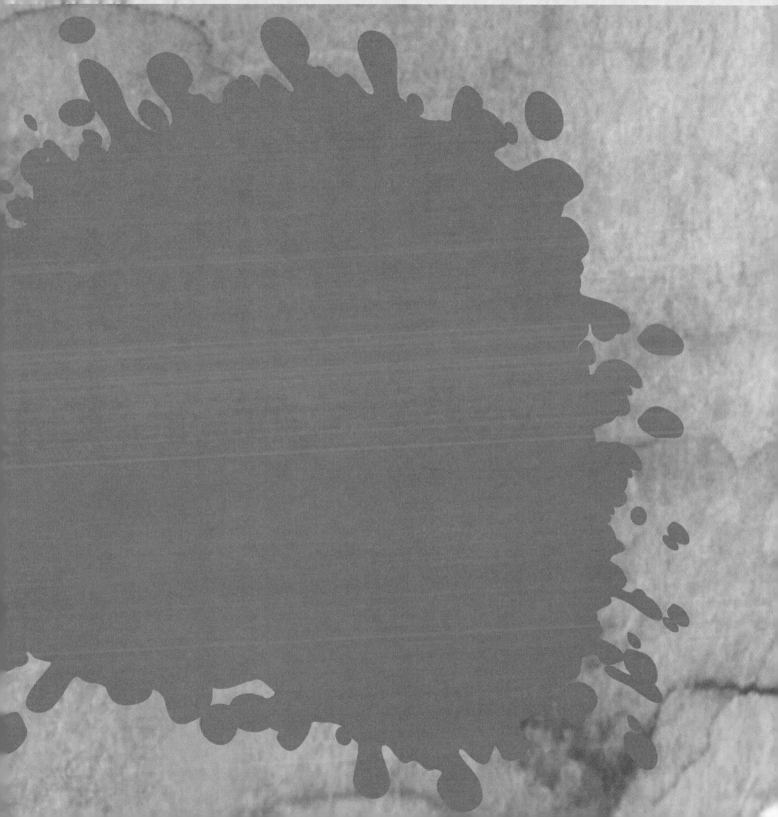

RED

Laal

लाल

Red is color of love, weddings and fertility; it is a mark of marriage. It is used to wish the Gods and Goddesses a Happy Holi.

YELLOW

Peela

पीला

Yellow symbolizes health and happiness. It is the color of knowledge and learning
It is also related to Vishnu.

BLUE

Neela

नीला

Blue represents the Lord Krishna. It is as symbol of the infinite and the immeasurable.

ORANGE

Narangi

नारंगी

Orange is color of the sun; it represents a new day.

GREEN

Hara

हरा

Green symbolizes new beginnings, harvest and fertility.

Saffron, red, yellow, blue, orange and green are the most important for the Holi festival.

Apart from that, we have other colors.

Let's see!

White

Safed
सफेद

It represents purity, cleanliness, peace and knowledge.

PINK

Gulabi

गुलाबी

Pink is a feminine color. It is associated with Goddess Lakshmi and represents her compassionate form – She is the mother to all living beings.

Purple

Baingani

बैंगनी

Purple is the color of oneness with god, peace and wisdom.

BROWN

Bhura

भूरा

Brown is often related to autumn, melancholy.

GREY

Dhumaila

धुमैला

Gray is the color of intellect and of compromise - it is between white and black.

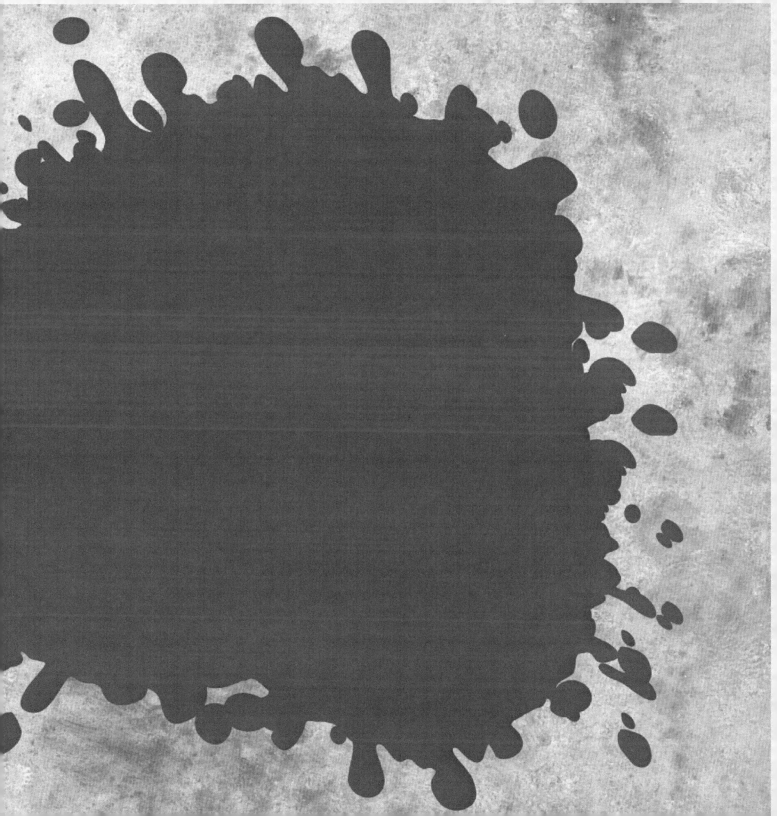

BLACK

Kaala

काला

Black is the color of anger and darkness.
in India it has connotations with evil and negativity.

Now we know all of the colors!

What is your favourite one?

Thank you for choosing our book.
We hope you spent a lovely time with it!

If you like our little book we would appreciate it
if you can share your opinion on Amazon.

If you want to receive
information about new books from series
or you have any suggestions for our future publications
please contact us:

amy.singh.amazon@gmail.com

SEE MORE
AMY SINGH'S BOOKS HERE:

Made in United States
North Haven, CT
03 March 2023

33492309R10020